The Successful

Presenter's

Handbook

by

Alan Matthews

An essential guide

to

business presentations

and

public speaking

The Successful Presenter's Handbook

by

Alan Matthews

ISBN: 978-1492171270

First Published 2013 by HLS Publishing Solutions

Praise for the Book

An excellent, clear analysis of how to prepare a first-rate presentation. I particularly like that Alan encourages us to distinguish between presenter notes, visual aids and a printed handout – they are too often one and the same. If I followed all his advice, I am certain that I would deliver an outstanding presentation.

Shabra Dowson

Very straight forward, readable and an essential book to have for any trainer or would be speaker.

Geoffrey Seaman

This new book on Presentations is excellent, well presented and covers all the salient points. I would certainly recommend this book to anyone who is looking to use PowerPoint during their training or talk. Really enjoyed the book, informative and enjoyable.

Heather Sheen

What can I say?! It's brilliant!

You have effectively highlighted the mistakes I think 99% of us make – using "PowerPoint" as a visual aid! All in all; a fabulous book – lovely light, friendly and accessible writing style; as if we're sitting together discussing presentations; you kept me interested and enthused throughout– and your advice and guidance will mean I shall be making changes to my presentations to renew my positivity about my work! Thank you!

Tammy Harper

Alan strips away the mystique of public speaking, replacing it with a pragmatic guide on how to grab the attention of audiences, get the message across and help them to understand and remember what they've been listening to .

His tips on really engaging the audience cover both how to overcome the presenter's nerves and the skills of building rapport with different types of groups.   Whether an occasional or regular speaker, this book will assist the reader to inspire and enthuse their audiences.

Maureen Lobatto

I really like the book. It's easy to read and there's nothing I would take out or add. I think you have covered all the bases. I recommend it to anyone planning their presentation and seeking straight talking words of wisdom on the subject.

Bill Husband

I thought your book was succinct, clear and concise. Although the book starts with very basic advice, I have sat through, and probably given, many poor presentations because these basic steps were overlooked. Well done. I will certainly recommend this book to my trainers and trainees.

Mair Hopkin

I have not had any training or teaching about delivering presentations and so like many others, I have learnt from my peers. Having read this book I now recognise where I am going wrong! A lot of it is common sense and quite obvious once you have pointed it out. This book is a very useful tool that anyone could use to prepare, plan and deliver an outstanding presentation! It is informative, gives good clear guidelines and addresses the inherent misconceptions so many of us have when delivering a presentation.

Lisa Pegg

Alan's book offers essential structure and practical steps to build a presentation and to deliver with confidence – even if you are a novice. The detailed tips and Alan's down to Earth narrative style make this a must-read for everyone who has to present professionally.

Nadine de Zoeten

I learned more from this book about giving presentations than the 'Training the Trainers' courses I have been on. It is so readable and user friendly and I have no doubt it will influence for the better any future presentations I give.

Denise Edwards

Alan is expert at helping others plan, develop and deliver an effective and memorable presentation. The book is written with practical, insightful and helpful steps to achieve your key goals from your presentation. I would recommend it to anyone who is starting to, or has been giving presentations as there is something there for everyone.

Julie Shehata-Morgan

Acknowledgements

My thanks to all the following who have given their time by reviewing drafts of this book, making helpful suggestions and spotting the inevitable typos and errors.

Heather Sheen, Geoffrey Seaman, Bill Husband, Nadine de Zoeten, Lisa Pegg, Colin Bates, Mair Hopkin, Shabra Dowson, Maureen Lobatto, Denise Edwards, Mary Lou McDermott, Julie Shehata-Morgan and Tammy Harper.

Thanks also to Helen Stothard of www.hlspublishing.com for her tireless efforts and good humour in getting this book published.

I should also thank all those speakers and presenters I have worked with and listened to over the years. Many of them have enthralled me with their skill and passion, showing me time and again the power that great speakers have to move and inspire an audience. They have given me something to aim for in constantly seeking to develop my own skills. Others have reduced me to tears of desperation and boredom and have driven me on to do what I can to change the world of business presentations. In that sense, this book owes something to both kinds of speaker.

And, most of all, thanks to my wife Catherine, without whom I would have no voice to speak and nothing worthwhile to say.

Contents

Introduction

Let's face it - there are too many tedious, irrelevant, pointless, unstructured, badly thought-out presentations going on in the world right now.

There are too many dull, uninspiring speakers delivering them.

There are too many bored, desperate people listening to them, looking at their watches and wishing they were somewhere else.

You don't want to be part of that, do you?

No, of course you don't. And neither do I.

That's why I'm so passionate about helping you to become a different kind of speaker. A speaker who is worth listening to. A speaker who has something worthwhile to say and can say it in a way which grabs attention and moves people.

If that's what you want as well, join the party and let's change the way presentations are done.

You may be a reluctant speaker, someone who would rather not bother at all but you have to because somehow it's become part of your job. So all you want is some basic information to help you do it reasonably well and not make an idiot of yourself.

Or you may be an enthusiastic speaker who really quite enjoys the experience. You're already a good speaker but you know you could be better. Either way, this book will help you.

This book gives you tips from the "inside". Tips which will help you to cut the time it takes learning to be a really good presenter. Tips which will save you making the mistakes most speakers make and will also save you from the stress and potential embarrassment of learning by trial and error.

Speaking is like any other skill. Cover the basics well and you'll do a good job. Master a few more advanced techniques and you can be outstanding – every time. Of course, as with any skill, you do need to practise. Reading won't make you a better speaker, experience will. But reading this book will make your experience easier, less traumatic and much more rewarding.

I've been a public speaker for 40 years. I've spoken to business meetings, professional conferences, client seminars, public meetings and countless training events. I've had to prepare and deliver hundreds of business presentations. I've found out the hard way what works and what doesn't. And I'm sharing all my experience in this book.

It takes you right through the process from start to finish. It doesn't go into a lot of background or theory. My guess is you don't really want that. You just want to know what to do.

The book covers all the fundamentals but it also reveals those crucial details that separate the professionals from the amateurs.

Dip into it, keep it with you, refer to it whenever you have to give a talk or a presentation. You may never need another book on public speaking.

Chapter One

The Ten Steps for Preparation

If you're like most of the people I work with, you're probably a part – time speaker and presenter. In other words, delivering presentations is just one aspect of your work and perhaps, in your eyes, not even the main part.

But, however you feel about it, you need to do it well. After all, you want to be a success. You want to make a good impression. Whether you're delivering business presentations, technical reports, academic talks or sales pitches, you need to be able to get a good result – every time.

One thing that will help you enormously is to have a clear and simple formula for preparing your talks, something you can follow to save you time, save you stress and make sure you're doing the right things in the right order.

But, if you only speak occasionally, or if presenting isn't the main part of what you do, there's a good chance that you haven't got that formula yet. You've probably found some things that work and some that don't, but it may be a bit hit and miss. Sometimes you get it right, sometimes you don't.

It's like having a recipe for baking a cake. If you follow the recipe the same way every time, you'll get the same result. If you try to make it up as you go along or to cut corners, you may get the occasional success, but you'll also get some disasters.

That's why I've come up with this 10 step guide to preparing powerful presentations. This is your recipe.

Make no mistake, many presentations start to go wrong from the very first stages. From the moment someone asks you to give a presentation, the next steps you take, and the order in which you take them, will determine whether or not it's a success.

Of course, delivery is critical as well. But, if you go wrong at the preparation stage, you'll be struggling when it comes to the delivery, however good a speaker you are.

Going back to the cake idea, if you miss out a step in your baking and your cake falls flat, you can dress it up with icing and fancy decorations but, when people eat it, they'll still know it's a disaster.

So here are my 10 steps to preparing powerful presentations. Later chapters will give you more details about each of the stages.

Step One: Find out about the audience

Many people, asked to give a talk, wonder just where to start.

This comes just after wondering, "Why me?" and, "How can I get out of this?"

Your very first thought should be to learn as much as you can about your audience:

- who are they?

- why do they need this talk?

- what are they expecting?

- what existing knowledge do they have?

- have they volunteered to come or have they been sent?

- how many people will be there?

- what happened to the last presenter who spoke to them?

The answers to these questions will determine your content and your approach – you can pick out the essentials for this particular audience. What do they need to know about this subject at this point? Why?

A lot of people try to prepare their talk without answering these questions.

The only questions they ask themselves are, "How much do I know about this topic? How much can I squeeze into the time available?"

They are heading for disaster.

This is why, as audiences, we sit through talks which have no relevance, talks which tell us what we already know or which are completely over our heads – because the speaker didn't take the trouble to find out what we needed.

If you've been asked to give the presentation by someone else, ask them the questions listed above. If you've decided to give the talk yourself, make sure you've thought them through so you're clear about what you're trying to achieve. Never assume that your audience understands what you're going to talk about or why.

They may have been told to turn up for the talk or may just have been given a title, with no real idea of what it will cover.

Try to find out how the talk is being promoted to your potential audience. This will give you a good idea of what they will be expecting and how you should pitch the talk.

Step Two: Think about your purpose

What is the point of this presentation? (It's better that you ask the question rather than your audience).

What is it meant to achieve, is it to:

- inform?

- train?

- motivate?

- persuade?

- sell?

- move people to action?

What do you want the audience to think, feel, know or do at the end? Why has someone asked you to deliver it?

If you think your presentation is just about "giving information", I'm afraid you're missing the point somewhere.

No presentation is just about passing on information. You can do that in an email or a report. Why do people need the information? How will they use it? How will it help them? And why do you need to take up everyone's time by standing there telling them about it?

Once you're clear about the answers to these questions, you can do a much better job of selecting the content for your talk and structuring it so that it achieves its objectives.

Be aware of 'hidden' purposes.

For example, you may be asked to give a presentation to some clients. The *explicit* purpose is to give them information about your organization.

But the *implicit* purposes may be to impress them, to build a rapport with them, to get them to like you, to show them how clever you are.

All these may have an impact on how you decide to deliver your presentation, what sort of content you cover and what other information you give them to take away.

Step Three: Check the timing

Find out how long you have to deliver the talk.

It's useful to know this before you start thinking about your content because, of course, it will have a big impact on how much you can cover.

How flexible is the timing you've been given? Sometimes the person organizing it has just made up a time. Find out more – what is the minimum and maximum time you have?

If they say, "you have an hour" does the talk have to be this long or do they just have an hour long space to fill?

What you should be thinking is, "What can I deliver in that time which is valuable to the audience and which achieves the purpose of the presentation?"

What you should NOT be thinking is," How much content can I cram into that time? What if I speak really fast? Can I sneak an extra few minutes on the end?"

I'll say more about this later but always aim to end before your time is up. Never go on beyond the time allowed.

In some circumstances, you may find that you have far less time than you expected. For example, if you're presenting to a Board of Directors as part of a meeting, be prepared to find that they're running late and may ask you to cover the highlights of your talk in 10 minutes rather than the 30 minutes you've prepared.

You also need to find out whether you're the only speaker or part of a panel. If there's a panel, how long is the whole event? What are the other people speaking about? Who are they?

Step Four: Develop the content

When you know about your audience and the purpose of your presentation you can start to put together the content.

Begin by brainstorming – let your mind run free, write down any ideas which come into your head. Don't analyse them or judge them at this stage, just work as quickly as you can and get as many ideas down as possible for points you could cover. Some people like neat, logical lists, other prefer mind maps or spider maps drawn out over a page or on a whiteboard. Others use Post It notes with key ideas on which they can arrange on a wall and move around. Try different methods and see what works best for you in producing the most ideas.

If you know the subject well, this will probably give you more than enough material to start with.

If you need more, do some research – look through some books or browse the Internet, talk to other people. There are plenty of sources of information to fill any gaps in your knowledge.

As you do your research, jot down notes of major areas or pieces of information you come across and add them to your plan as you go so you can see where they fit into the bigger picture.

I guarantee – after this exercise you will have far too much possible content. Cut it down.

You will still have too much. Cut it down again. Seriously.

Be ruthless in stripping out content. This is where knowing your audience and having a clear sense of purpose are vital. What is the *essential* content your audience needs from you to make the talk worthwhile?

In fact, if you could use just one sentence to summarise the key point you want to make in your presentation, what would it be? That's the core of your message and everything else is there to support it.

Remember – it's not about showing them how much you know, it's about giving them what they need. If you find it hard to select the right content and to cut it down, it probably means you're not clear enough about the audience and the purpose. You may need to go back and ask some more questions.

Do not overload your talk with too much material. This is one of the most common mistakes presenters make.

See the chapter on content and structure for more detail on how to select the right content for your group.

Step Five: Plan the structure

Now put your content into a clear structure.

Break the content down into small sections with key points in each. This framework will help you to work out the timings for the talk. Remember to allow time for your introduction and conclusion and for any questions.

Make sure the structure flows clearly and logically from one stage to the next.

As with content, don't have too many steps, probably 3 main sections.

For example, you could use Past/Present/Future, Position/Problem/Proposal, Why/How/What or you could use a story structure to help your material flow.

You can use this outline as your "big picture" introduction so your audience knows where you're going with the talk. You can also use it as the basis for your own notes to keep you on track.

Combining the content and the structure means you now have the presentation mapped out in detail.

When you have the framework, make sure you plan a clear opening section and a powerful ending. See the chapter on content and structure for more ideas.

Step Six: Spice it up - think about visual aids, etc.

Consider whether you need visual aids to support your key points. Notice that you do not consider visual aids until after you've thought about all the other points above. That's because, until you've thought about those things, you don't know whether you will need any visual aids.

And, by visual aids, I don't mean PowerPoint slides with words on which you also plan to use as your own notes or as handouts. Do you really need me to explain why that's so wrong? If you do, I go into more detail in the chapter on How to Use Visual Aids Effectively.

Visual aids should be big, bold and simple. They should add impact, aid understanding and support your key points. In other words, they should be VISUAL and AIDS. Read the chapter on How to Use Visual Aids Effectively for more ideas.

Don't just think about slides or flipcharts, you can also use video clips, DVDs, props, objects, people – so long as they are there for a purpose.

You can also plan where to use stories, case studies, practical activities, examples or interactive elements to break up the talk and add emphasis to your key points. All these things can be used to add interest and to bring your presentation to life. But they have to support the purpose of your talk.

Of course, this step often goes in tandem with some of the earlier steps. While you're thinking about your content and your structure, you'll be thinking about places where visuals or other aids can fit in.

But the visuals, and other elements, are driven by the content, not the other way round.

Having said that, you may find at times that you come up with a really powerful visual which can act as a centrepiece, or even a metaphor, around which you can build your presentation. In that case, you may go back and revise your notes to fit around it.

Step Seven: Write your own notes

Now use the content and the structure to prepare your own notes if you need them, on cards or on paper, to help you stay on track.

Make them brief - just notes, not a script. You want the delivery to be as natural as possible, as if you're having a conversation with your audience. Writing a script will lead you to use more formal language. If you read from a script, you won't be able to make a real connection with your audience and, if you try to memorise a script, you'll put yourself under even more pressure, trying to remember the exact words. It's usually better to be clear about the key points you want to make and think of some good phrases to use.

However, there are two sections of your talk which you really should plan, memorise and rehearse. These are your opening and closing remarks. These are the points where you will have the greatest impact and you shouldn't leave them to chance.

Step Eight: Anticipate questions

Now is a good time to think again about the questions your audience might ask.

You should have done this to some extent already when preparing your material but now that you have your content planned, what other questions might arise which you haven't covered? Plan for these and prepare your answers.

You know that one question you hope no-one will ask? That's the one you need to think about.

You should also decide when you will take questions – will you have a Q & A session at the end or do you want people to ask questions as you go along?

Step Nine: Write any handouts

Decide whether you want to supply handouts for the audience.

These could include summaries of your key points, further content or more detailed information which they can take away and read later. If so, what form will they take and when will you give them out?

As well as having materials which they might read later, consider having something to use as they go along to help them follow the talk, perhaps to fill in, make notes on or do something with to make the presentation more interactive.

Step Ten: Rehearse

Rehearse the talk in some way.

How you do this will depend on your own preference but you should have some form of run through to check timings and to get some ideas for the best way to put certain points across.

Some people find they rehearse in their head as they're doing other things, others stand and give the talk to themselves, their loved ones, a close family pet, a tape recorder or a video camera.

I disagree with some people who suggest you practice while looking in a mirror. I find that too distracting and unnatural.

When you work out timings, remember to allow more time for interactive elements, including Q & A.

If you're going to use equipment, practice with it first.

Make sure you're confident about handling any computers, projectors, microphones, etc.

If possible, have a look at the room and get a feel for it.

If not, at least ask about the size and layout. Check the position of all exits and whether the audience will be between you and the doors .

Check who's responsible for setting everything up, for putting out the chairs and equipment, for printing off and distributing handouts, etc. Don't assume that someone else will do all these things for you.

Work out what could possibly go wrong and plan for it. This is a good way to calm your nerves and to make sure you can deal with anything that might arise.

Summary – follow this 10 step process whenever you're asked to give a talk or presentation:

- Audience

- Purpose

- Timing

- Content

- Structure

- Visual aids

- Notes

- Questions

- Handouts

- Rehearse

No, it doesn't spell out a handy acronym, but it does work!

Chapter Two

How To Choose The Right Content And Structure

Find a good title

You do want people to come to your presentation, don't you?

A good title will increase interest and also give people a good idea what to expect, so there's less chance of them being disappointed because they came along expecting something different.

So, if you have the chance to come up with your own title, make it something interesting which also tells people what benefit they'll get from attending.

Titles including, "How to..." and "...Tips..." always work well.

For example, instead of a boring, generic title like "Time Management, try:

- How To Save An Hour A Day or

- 6 Top Tips for Getting More Done

As well as encouraging people to come, titles like these also give you a ready – made structure for your talk.

If you're giving a very technical presentation, as I used to do on Tax topics, you can still choose a title which shows exactly what you're talking about and attracts the right people. For example:

- A beginner's guide to Inheritance Tax

- 6 ways to pay less Capital Gains Tax

- Business owners – what to do when the VAT man calls

Select the essential content

Keep the content simple, clear and concise.

Always ask yourself:

"What does this particular audience need to know about this topic at this particular time"

NOT

"How much information can I squeeze into the time available to show how much I know about this topic?"

Remember – it is always about your audience, not about you.

Your primary aim is to give your audience something of value, something they can take away, remember and use. Your primary aim is not to make yourself look clever or to impress people with how much you know.

There are 3 categories of information:

1. The essential content that this audience *must* know to make the presentation worthwhile and for it to achieve its purpose

2. Other information it might be useful for them to know if there's time or if questions arise, but which isn't essential

3. Information which they really don't need at this point.

Guess which you should include in your talk?

Build your presentation around Category 1 and leave out everything else.

If you have time, prepare some Category 2 information so you have it ready if needed, in case someone asks you about it or if you've underestimated the level of your audience and you need something a bit more advanced. But don't mention it unless you really have to and don't let it get in the way of your essential content.

Category 3? This has no place in your presentation, even if someone asks you about it. You don't want to take people's time up on it and it may only confuse some of your audience. This is where you say, "Sorry, that's outside the scope of what I want to cover today. Can I talk to you about it separately?"

I've sometimes found, when preparing a presentation, that it was very difficult deciding which content was essential and which should be left out. In those situations, it has *always* been because I wasn't clear enough about who my audience would be and why they needed the information.

If you're finding it hard to make decisions about what to keep and what to leave out, go back to basics and ask yourself why you're giving this presentation in the first place. Who will be there and what do they need to get out of it?

If you can't answer that question because you think your audience will be mixed in terms of their knowledge or experience, e.g. both junior and senior people from an organisation, then you really need to ask why those people will be there. Do they really all need to attend the presentation? If so, what do they expect to get from it? Do they all have a realistic expectation of what the presentation will cover and how it will help them?

Giving your presentation a clear title will help you to limit its scope so that people can determine whether it will be of use to them or not. But you may still find that people turn up who are not really the target audience. This may be because everyone has been told they have to come or just because it's happening at lunchtime and there are free sandwiches (I'm not joking, a lot of my training presentations were at lunchtimes and I don't mind admitting that the presence of a free lunch made a big difference in terms of the numbers who turned up for them).

I still maintain that you have to be clear about the scope of your talk and who it is mainly aimed at. If other people then turn up, they have to accept that they may not get as much value from it as the people it was designed for.

For instance, I used to do some technical presentations which were mainly for junior staff but some very senior staff would come - not just for the lunch, but to make sure they hadn't missed anything important. They saw it as a quick refresher.

I still explained that the talk would be aimed at the less experienced people there and I wouldn't be going into great detail or discussing advanced issues. (Those would be in Category 3 above - outside the scope of the talk).

If you can't avoid having a mixed audience, you need to decide which section of that audience is most important to you - because it's very unlikely that you can keep everyone happy. When you try to include something for everyone, you end up including too much information, you lose focus and everyone ends up dissatisfied.

Be ruthless in stripping out content

Repeat the following sentence until it is fixed firmly in your head and can only be removed by surgical intervention:

"The amount you say does not equal the amount the audience takes in."

Here's an exercise – take a glass. Hold it under a tap and turn on the water. Let the tap keep running. What happens? Does the glass miraculously expand to take in all the water?

No.

Well, the human brain is just like that. It doesn't expand to take in all the content you pour in. It just overflows. Do your audience a favour and be ruthless!

Be prepared to cut out a section of your talk if you're running out of time rather than rushing through the material.

It will look more organised and most people won't notice that you missed anything out. When you prepare the talk, think about which areas you could cut down if this happened.

This will also help if you find you have to cut the time for delivering the presentation. It's not unusual for a presenter to prepare a 60 minute talk, for instance, and suddenly be asked, "Actually, we're running a bit late. Can you cut it down to 30 minutes?"

If you've done your homework and you're very clear about your target audience and the central purpose of the talk, you'll be able to give an "executive summary" at that point and, believe me, people will be far more impressed than if you try to rush through masses of information in a short time, leaving them confused and shell-shocked.

Plan your structure

Decide on a logical structure or flow for the talk.

The content of your presentation may suggest its own structure, depending on its purpose.

For example, if you're giving information about something, you may clearly need to cover A before B or it won't make any sense.

Have you ever got to the punch line of a joke and then realised you missed out something earlier on? " Oh yes, I should have mentioned – the man in the car had a wooden leg. "

Then you'll understand how important it can be to get the information in the right order before you start.

As a rule, try to move from the general to the specific, from big picture to detail.

Give people a broad view of the area you're covering before going into the finer points.

I've seen many speakers ignore this point and completely lose their audience in the first 5 minutes.

Depending on your topic, there are various structures you could consider. Here are some examples.

problem/solution

This can be useful for sales presentations. For example:

Problem – your current database doesn't allow you to organise client details by geographical region.

Solution – our software allows you to do this easily by…

present situation/future situation

Example:

Present situation - we have two different departments dealing with staffing and recruitment matters.

Future situation – we're going to reorganise into one department with this structure…

question/answer

Example:

Question – how can we provide an outstanding service to our clients?

Answer – by always exceeding their expectations. And we do this by…

position/problem/possibilities/proposal

Example:

Position – at the moment we operate from two separate buildings

Problem – this causes confusion amongst clients and it makes communication difficult between departments

Possibilities – carry on as we are, keep both buildings but change the way departments are situated, close one building and try to fit into the other one, close both buildings and lease a larger one

Proposal – my proposal is that we close both buildings and lease a larger one when something suitable becomes available.

Break up the content into sections with their own key points and their own brief openings and endings.

Using any of the structures above will help you with this as your sections will be very clear.

This makes the talk easier to follow and easier for you to remember. It also allows you to summarise and repeat the key points naturally.

When you deliver the presentation, make the structure clear by having a "map" at the start, showing where you're going.

Remind people at regular points exactly where you are and where you're going next. Link the sections of the talk with short phrases such as, "Now we've looked at X, let's move on to have a look at Y".

Open with impact

Make sure you plan clear opening and closing sections for the talk.

People remember most from the start and the end (in fact, these may be the only parts some people hear) so these are the times when you'll have most impact.

The first thing you need to do is to grab the audience's attention. You can do this by using:

- a quotation

- a (relevant) story

- an interesting fact or statistic

- a rhetorical question

NEVER start with a joke unless you're a very good stand up comedian and the joke is relevant.

A joke that falls flat will make you wish you were somewhere else, and your audience will feel the same.

Then there are certain things you will need to cover in the early parts of the talk.

When an audience faces a presenter, they have these questions in their minds:

- what is this going to be about exactly?

- what use is it going to be to me?

- is this going to be a waste of my time?

- is this speaker any good?

- will it be interesting?

You need to answer those questions right at the start.

Of course, you do this partly by having an opening with impact, as I mentioned above. Also by looking as if you know what you're doing, by appearing to be confident and competent. This is why you need to know exactly what you're going to say at the start, so you can create the best impression.

When you're planning the talk, work out a couple of sentences to explain why *you* are just the right person to be giving this talk so you can mention it at the beginning.

This is even more important if you're only doing it because someone told you to do it. You may need to convince *yourself* first.

Of course, you can take a few moments to set out who you are and what your experience is. But this can be a bit tedious, to be honest. I've sat through a lot of speakers who started off by giving a long list of their supposed achievements or their job titles.

There's a great American speaker called Larry Wingett (known as "the pit bull of personal development"). He once said he refused to open his talks with a list of what he had done because, "You don't really care who I was or how good I used to be. You just care whether the next 45 minutes is going be a worthwhile use of your time."

I think he's right. People just want to feel confident that you know what you're talking about and you're going to deliver it in a way that's interesting and useful.

So, if you're going to mention your background, keep it brief and relevant.

"I'm speaking today because I built my own IT business from scratch and sold it for £5 million last year."

"I've been involved in sales for over 20 years and I've trained hundreds of people to use the same successful techniques I've used myself."

A better way to let people know that you're worth listening to is to weave your experience into the early stages of the talk. You can do this by using stories and examples which reveal the extent of your knowledge in a rather more subtle fashion than simply listing your achievements or telling people your job title.

So, in the opening section of your presentation, clarify:

- what you're talking about

- what benefit the audience will get from it

- who you are and what you know about the subject and

- start with an overview before going into detail

Also, tell them how long the talk is going to last and whether you'll be allowing questions.

However, I would suggest using your opening quotation, story or whatever *before* covering these points. Your main aim at the start is to grab people's attention.

Don't waste the key opening seconds telling people your name and reminding them of the title of your presentation – they probably already know this.

For example, here's one opening:

"Good afternoon, ladies and gentlemen. Thank you for coming along to this talk today. My name is Alan Matthews and I'm going to talk to you for 30 minutes on the topic of Effective Meetings."

That's fairly typical (not of me, honestly, just other people). Not very gripping, is it?

How about this instead?

"How much time do you spend every week in meetings?

It's been estimated that the typical manager spends 30% of his or her time in meetings. That's maybe 13 hours a week – nearly 2 days. How much of that time do you think they spend wishing they were somewhere else?

Well, in the next 30 minutes I'm going to tell you 4 ways to cut the time you spend in useless meetings."

I think that has a bit more punch to it, don't you?

Famous last words – prepare your closing remarks

Plan your close when preparing the talk (after all, this may be the part you're looking forward to most).

In fact, you should really work back from your close, building the rest of the presentation around that.

Why? Because, presumably, at the close, you'll aim to achieve the purpose of the whole talk - a clear summary of your key points, a statement, a question or a call to action which has some impact.

What's the one thing you want your audience to remember, to do or to feel when you've finished?

What you leave your audience with at the end should be a culmination of all that has gone before it. So it makes some sense to start by thinking, "What do I want to leave them with?" Then work backwards, making sure that all your other content and structure leads up to that point effectively.

Whatever you do, don't let your ending be a massive disappointment, as many are.

Don't just say, " Well, that's about it...unless there are any questions? " – give your close the same impact as the opening.

You may even want to refer back to the quotation, statistic or question you used at the start to give the talk a feeling of completeness.

Decide whether you're going to allow questions at the end or just head for the door as soon as you've finished speaking.

If you do take questions, allow time for them and then have another short summary of your key points to round things off so the talk doesn't just fizzle out.

There's more information about this in the chapter on How To Handle Questions.

A good talk should be like a good film. It leaves people talking about it when they go out. A bad one leaves them talking about how to get home or where they parked the car.

It's all in the timing

A lot of people who are new to presenting worry about not having enough material. They tend to think that they won't be able to fill the time available. That's partly why they include too much content.

In my experience the opposite is true. Most speakers have far too much material and are wildly unrealistic about how much they can, and should, try to cover in the tine they have.

When considering your timing, think about how many areas you're covering in your talk and how many key points you have to make.

Don't forget the opening and ending sections.

If your talk is to last an hour, let's say, and you have 3 main sections, then you might allow:

- 5 minutes for an opening section

- 3 minutes for a closing section

- 10 minutes for questions, leaving

- 14 minutes each for your main sections

If each of your main sections has 3 key points, then you have less than 5 minutes for each key point.

This simple calculation can save you from wild overestimates about how much you can cover in the time.

Never go over your allotted time. Never.

It's one of the worst things you can do. Always aim to end a bit short. If you're given an hour to speak, prepare for 50 minutes. No-one will complain that they've been short-changed because you've finished a bit early.

On the other hand, everyone will resent it if you run over your time and keep them there longer than they expected. The people in your audience are busy, they have other things to do. Going on too long is simply poor time management.

As I mentioned earlier, if you look like running out of time, leave out some section of the talk rather than rushing to get through everything.

Keeping to time is especially important if there are other speakers going on after you. It's extremely disrespectful and unprofessional to run into their time because you haven't managed your own.

Plan some interaction

When you're planning, look for opportunities to involve people by asking them questions, getting them to offer ideas, letting them talk to each other, etc.

See the chapter on How to Really Engage Your Audience for suggestions.

Chapter Three

How To Prepare And Use Notes

When I ask people on my courses what they're afraid of when they have to speak, most say, "forgetting what I'm going to say".

Another common fear is, "getting a question I don't know the answer to".

These are interesting, because:

a) neither happens anywhere near as often as you might think,

and

b) both situations are easy to prepare for and deal with.

I deal with handling questions in another chapter, but here are some ideas for making sure you don't forget what you want to say.

The simplest way to keep yourself on track is to use some basic notes.

Not exactly ground – breaking advice, is it?

But I do mean basic notes. The mistake many people make is that they don't trust the idea of keeping things simple and, instead, prepare pages of detailed, closely typed notes or even a written script.

Using a script

As a general rule, don't read from a script of your talk, don't even start with one as a way of preparing.

There are three main reasons.

Firstly, written language always uses more formal words and structures than spoken language. It's very difficult to write in a conversational style, which is what you need to be aiming for in most cases.

So, when you come to speak the words you've written down, it will tend to sound stilted and unnatural.

Secondly, if you try to memorise a script, this will actually put you under more pressure as you'll easily lose track if something interrupts your flow, e.g. a question.

I've seen a lot of people become flustered because they were trying to remember the exact word they'd written down when it didn't really matter anyway. If they hadn't been tied to a script, they would have thought of another word which would have done just as well.

Thirdly, if you actually read from a script, as well as sounding more formal, it will tend to restrict your eye contact and break your connection with the audience. It will make you far more likely to deliver in the style of a lecture than to give an engaging talk which keeps people's attention.

Again, if you're an experienced speaker, you may be able to handle a script. Some politicians, for example, can deliver a speech from a script very well. But to do so successfully, you really need a lot of experience, a lot of charisma, or a good speechwriter.

The main instances where people do need to read from a script are where the speech is to be sent out as a Press Release or quoted in some way (or where it is actually written by someone else), e.g. many major political speeches.

If you *have* to say something word for word, e.g. reading a quote or an extract, make this clear by picking up the paper and reading from it. This will highlight the fact that you're NOT reading out the rest of your talk and it will show your concern for accuracy when it matters.

Using notes

Notes should be just a reminder of your key topics and points and should be as brief as possible.

They need to be easily accessible and easily visible from a distance.

Break up your talk into smaller sections and break up each section into key points.

This will give you the framework and be the basis for your notes. The section headings and the list of key points for each may be the only notes you need.

You can type these out in large print on a piece of paper and have the paper somewhere handy so that you can see the notes easily when glancing down.

Alternatively, you could have the notes on the screen of your laptop or tablet placed where you can see it.

I try to keep any notes to a single page to save turning pages over. This means I don't have to touch the notes at all, just glance at them. This isn't always possible, of course, but I prefer it if I can do it.

I also mark timings for each section and the places where I want to use a flipchart or slide.

Don't put the paper close to a computer, projector or anything else which may blow air out and send your notes flying around the room.

Use cards if you find this easier than paper but remember that this may restrict your eye contact and hand movements.

Number the cards and keep them together by punching a hole in each one and tying them with a treasury tag or ring.

As I mention in the chapter on visual aids, DO NOT use slides as your own notes.

This will encourage you to look at the screen while you're speaking. It will also make the slides useless as visual aids. And if the projector breaks down you'll lose your notes.

If you're using a flipchart, one trick is to write a couple of words lightly on the corner of a page so that you can see them when you're turning the page over and remind yourself of the next point. The audience won't be able to see these.

Consider using PowerPoint Speaker Notes if you use slides.

These can be printed off to give you a small picture of the slide and bullet points next to it.

Alternatively, print off a copy of your slides (PowerPoint lets you select a Handout option for printing, which allows you to choose how many slides you want on a page) and write your notes next to each slide. This helps you to remember what's coming up on the screen.

Stop and look at your notes if you get lost or really forget where to go.

Taking a few seconds to get back on track gives a better impression than stumbling on when you don't know what to say next.

It's not a sign of weakness that you occasionally have to consult your notes. People will appreciate the fact that you have actually planned the talk and that you're concerned about getting it right.

Chapter Four

How To Calm Your Nerves

What are nerves?

Nerves are Nature's way of telling you that you're excited about something.

Well, that's one interpretation. Another could be that nerves are Nature's way of telling you to grab your coat and run.

But my point about being excited isn't just a flippant one. When you're really excited, how do you feel? Your heart beats faster, your palms get a bit sticky, your eyes dilate, the blood starts pumping, you get a funny feeling in your stomach, you may even tremble slightly.

Those are exactly the same symptoms as you get when you're nervous. Your body is doing the same thing, you're just interpreting it differently.

Nerves (and excitement) are really just the result of adrenalin pumping through your body. It's a natural reaction to certain situations, such as high excitement or stress – and most people find speaking in public stressful. Even experienced speakers still feel some nerves, they just know how to handle them.

What happens as you gain more experience is not that you lose the nerves altogether (although they do reduce as you get more practice) but that you realise the nerves needn't stop you doing a good job.

Instead of fighting the nerves and thinking, "Oh no, I'm nervous again. I can't do this", you just recognise and accept them as the usual sign that you're about to do something mildly stressful – then you get on with it. In fact, you may even start to interpret the signs as excitement rather than stress.

Here are some tips to help you to stay calm before a talk and to handle the nerves if they do arise.

Go through everything one more time before you start.

Feeling in control and knowing what you're doing is the best way to stay calm. That's why you need to turn up well before the start, so you don't feel rushed and you don't have any last minute surprises.

Work out exactly what you're going to say when you first stand up.

One of the few parts of your presentation that you should memorise is the opening. Unfortunately, the start, when you'll have the greatest impact and you'll be making that all-important first impression, is also the time when you'll be feeling most nervous. So know exactly what you're going to say when you stand up and don't change it at the last minute.

Don't tell the audience that you're nervous.

Some inexperienced presenters start by telling the audience how nervous they are. That's a big mistake.

Usually, the audience can't tell. Even if they can, they'll forgive some nerves, they know what it's like and they're just thankful it's not them having to do it. But telling them you're nervous doesn't get them on your side. It alerts them to look for the signs of nerves which you've just warned them about and it puts them on guard to expect a poor performance.

Avoid certain things which may emphasise your nerves.

Try to avoid holding thin sheets of paper or cards which may shake or using a remote control with tiny buttons. If you stand behind a lectern, don't grasp the sides with white knuckles looking as if you'll keel over if you let go.

Have a Plan B in case anything goes wrong.

Let's face it, you've probably been lying awake anyway thinking of all the things that could go wrong so why not turn it into a positive thing and have a back-up plan?

What do you think might go wrong? How can you try to prevent this? What will you do if this happens? Thorough preparation, and having a Plan B in case of a mishap, will help to keep you calm.

Remember that people want you to do well.

Most people will be glad it's not them having to speak and they'll respect you for doing it. They'll give you a chance to do well. If you come across as someone who is really trying to do your best for them, they'll accept a few flaws in your performance.

Believe it or not, the audience is nervous as well at the start. People are wondering whether this is going to be any good, whether you'll be worth listening to, whether it's all a waste of their time. They need you to help them settle down by showing that you're competent. So do the basic things that you need to do at the start so that everyone (including yourself) has a chance to settle down and relax.

Go through some relaxation exercises before the talk.

A few deep breathing exercises can be a big help.

Breathe in deeply from your stomach, inhale through your nose and slowly exhale through your mouth. This will help to relax you and will also make your voice sound more powerful when you speak (when we get nervous, we tend to take shallow breaths from the chest and this restricts the flow of air, which makes the voice sound thin and weak).

It might help to do some gentle warm-up exercises before you start, just to loosen you up. Roll your shoulders, stretch your legs, swing your arms around.

Just remember to do this away from the audience, not when you're standing there waiting to go on. Otherwise you'll look like a boxer.

Mingle

If you can, mingle with the people arriving for the talk and speak to some of them.

If I'm speaking at a large venue, I love to stand at the front and watch the room fill up as people come in. It gives me a real buzz and gets me fired up to start speaking. I've spoken to actors who do the same thing. There's probably a medical term for it.

Most people would find that idea horrifying and it would be more likely to induce vomiting than to get them in the right frame of mind.

An alternative is, where possible, to mingle with people as they come in. Talk to some of them, especially people you know. This will break the ice and make it seem less like "you and them". But make sure everything is ready first so you can stay calm.

Appear Confident

Remember that it's more important to **appear** confident than to actually **be** confident.

When you're feeling nervous, you look at other people and think, "They seem so calm, so confident." That's because you're comparing your inside to their outside. You're comparing how you feel with how they look.

People don't know how you feel, they only know how you look. If you look calm and confident, they'll assume that you really are calm and confident.

That's another reason not to tell people that you're nervous.

Smile, maintain eye contact and speak with enthusiasm – these are the key ways to appear confident and hide your nerves. Most people who look calm are just bluffing and you can as well.

Don't expect perfection.

Some things may go wrong, it's not the end of the world. And it's less likely if you're well prepared. Unless you're a professional speaker, you're only aiming at giving a good performance, not a great one.

If you do make a mistake, just carry on. Most people won't even notice. Don't react to it and don't think, "There you go, I knew I'd mess this up."

Keep things in perspective.

Very few audiences physically assault the speaker and you can probably sue them if they do.

Get the audience involved wherever possible.

There are lots of reasons for making your talk interactive, which I go through later. One good reason is that it breaks up the talk and takes the attention off you for a while. It also makes it feel more like a conversation than a presentation and you're not scared of a conversation are you?

Talk to yourself in a positive way before you start.

People are really good at talking themselves into a panic. They think about everything which could go wrong. They run through pictures in their minds of everything falling to pieces. They have this negative commentary running in their heads, telling them it's all a mistake, why do they think they can do this, what will happen if...

Why not flip it around and tell yourself that you know what you're doing, you're well prepared and you know that you can do this. Why shouldn't it go well? What happens if it's a huge success and everyone loves it? Just think how pleased you'll be.

Instead of imagining catastrophe, take time to visualise a scene where you're giving the talk and things are going really well. People are listening, laughing, applauding and you're feeling great.

Remember a time when you felt confident

Remember a time when you felt confident or when you did something really well.

Close your eyes and see the picture of you being successful. Try to recreate that feeling. Make it as real as possible. What can you see? What can you hear? What can you smell? As you see the picture, let your mouth spread into a huge smile.

Then pinch your thumb and finger together as you see the image.

This is called "anchoring". The more times you run through the picture and pinch your thumb and finger together, the more you will associate that physical act with that feeling, until you can pinch your thumb and finger together before you go on to speak and feel the confidence flowing through you.

Find a routine that puts you in a positive frame of mind.

This is a bit like the anchoring I mentioned above.

Many sports people, actors and other performers develop a standard routine which they go through in exactly the same way each time. It gets them "in the zone". A similar routine for you as a speaker might include doing a few breathing exercises, getting your notes in order, checking your slides, walking round the room where you're speaking to get a feel for it, running through your first few words and visualising a tremendous reception.

If you have some favourite music that stirs you or calms you, play it on your way to the talk. You might prefer some pounding Rock music to wind you up or some relaxing classical music to calm you down, whatever works for you.

Chapter
Five

How To Use Visual Aids Effectively

Why use visual aids?

Let's get something straight right from the start. There is no legal requirement for presenters to use visual aids.

I say this because some presenters seem to think that it's compulsory to project something onto a screen when they're speaking. That's the only reason I can think of to account for some of the appalling slides I've seen over the years.

You should only use a visual aid if it:

- adds impact to what you're saying

- helps people to understand a point

- creates interest

- explains something more effectively than words could by themselves.

Many slides I've seen do none of these things. That's because they're not really visual aids at all. They're the presenter's notes. Or they're the handouts for the audience prepared in PowerPoint.

This is so wrong I hardly know where to start (but I will mention it again later).

I think it might be easier to explain how to use visual aids if I cover some of the most common mistakes I've seen people make and show some examples.

I'll refer to slides here for simplicity, and because most presenters do use slides of some sort, but the principles apply to other visual aids as well.

Mistake 1: Hiding behind the visual aids

As a speaker, YOU are meant to be the focus of everyone's attention. Some of us love that (I know, it's weird), many people hate it. But it's true. Get used to it.

A presentation is not meant to be a slideshow with a voiceover.

But that's what far too many of them are. The speaker hides in the shadows with a remote, clicking through the slides, mumbling a few words as they pass by, hoping that the audience will be too engrossed in the slideshow to pay much attention to the person in the corner.

People want to see and hear *you*. They want a real human being in front of them, talking to them, doing your best to communicate with them and give them something worthwhile. They'll forgive many things if they see that you're trying to do that. What they won't forgive is your trying to hide behind the slides. That shows a complete lack of regard for them.

Mistake 2: Using slides as your own notes or as handouts

Have you ever sat through a presentation which mainly consisted of someone reading out the slides or listened to a speaker who spent most of the time with his or her back to you, checking what was on the screen?

If you haven't, then think yourself lucky. Some of us have wasted valuable hours of our lives, time we will never get back, doing just that.

If you have, then you know what it feels like and you should never think about putting other people through the same experience.

It happens because some speakers use the slides as their own notes.

I've even heard people on Presentation Skills courses say, "I need the slides to help me stay on track."

No. No. No. That's not what they're for.

They're supposed to be visual aids, not notes. They're supposed to help the audience, not you. If you need notes, write some on a piece of paper and keep them near you. Don't write them in PowerPoint and project them onto a screen behind you.

Slides are not handouts either. They're not meant to be printed off and read later. They're not meant to make sense to anyone who wasn't at the presentation. If you want handouts with information for people to take away, write some.

Visual aids, notes and handouts are three quite separate things with distinct purposes. You can't have one thing which combines all three.

I know you may be pressed for time when you're preparing your presentation but trying to make your slides do three jobs is just a lazy shortcut which shows a disregard for your audience.

Mistake 3: Only thinking of visual aids as slides

Most business presentations still involve PowerPoint. There are other programs which are becoming popular, such as Prezi or Keynote, but the point is that, when most presenters think of visual aids they think of slides.

Of course, there are some good reasons to use slides, whichever program you choose. They are easy to see, they can include dramatic visuals with massive impact (which is why it's such a crime to see them used primarily to project words on the screen).

But remember that there are alternatives. For example:

- interactive whiteboards

- static whiteboards or flipcharts

- actual objects and props

- DVDs or video clips

- people

- photographs

- cartoons

- puppets (yes, really, I've used them)

And, of course, your biggest visual aid is YOU. You're the one they're going to see most of (unless you're hiding in the corner, as I described earlier). So your own expression, stance, body language and energy will have a massive impact on how well you get your message across.

Mistake 4: Using too many slides with words on

I've mentioned already about not using slides as your own notes.

In fact, you should really avoid using many slides which just have words on. Words are not visual and people don't remember them. Words on a screen don't add to the words you're saying yourself and, if you show words and carry on talking, people are torn between listening to you or reading the slide. In fact, they may well decide to do neither.

One exception to the suggestion about not using slides with words on would be where you have something like a quotation, a statement or a formula which you want to put up and comment on.

Even then, it might have more impact if you can show a relevant image alongside the words.

A common mistake is to show a series of bullet point slides. These are very easy to produce in PowerPoint, which is one reason why some presenters use them so much. It's easy and it's quick.

There's also a misconception that, if you have several points to make, putting them together in bullet point form (especially if you build them up one by one) helps the audience to focus on them and remember them.

In my experience, if people see a bullet point slide, they will usually only glance at it, then look away and they probably won't remember what the points were a few seconds later.

Rather than use a bullet point slide with several items on, work out what your key message is and show that in a bold and simple way, then bring out any supporting points in your talk.

STRESSED?

Get

Help!

One place where people tend to show a bullet point slide is at the start, where they will show a list of the topics to be covered.

Managing Performance

- Why it is important for you to manage people's performance

- What people lack – reasons why people may be underperforming

- What people need from you – the 3 things which you need to deliver as a manager

It's certainly helpful to set out the scope of your talk at the start so people know what you're going to cover. But starting off with a boring bullet point list doesn't set great expectations for the rest of the presentation.

If you do want to show a slide to give an outline of the talk, why not at least try to find something a bit different, such as a simple graphic like this?

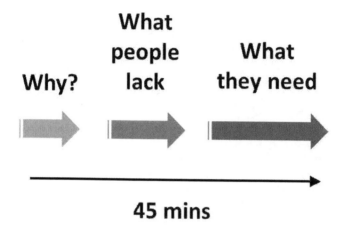

Mistake 5: Showing pictures which add nothing to the point being made

Another common mistake is to use pictures which don't really add or explain anything, they just illustrate a word. For example:

Getting More Out Of Your Laptop

These sorts of slides do have their uses. They can be useful transitions from one point to another. The change of the slide at least indicates that something is happening, we're moving on. But they don't have a lot of impact and, if they're overused, they will become tedious very quickly. People will stop looking because they know the picture isn't going to add anything.

It's more effective to use an image which adds some humour, shows the audience a situation they can relate to, acts as a metaphor or makes people think a little to see the connection.

Getting More Out Of Your Laptop

Mistake 6: Using all the animations and transitions

Some presenters get a little over-excited about all the bells and whistles in PowerPoint, Prezi or whichever programme they're using.

They discover you can make the slides whizz in from one side, drop in from the top or dissolve. You can make words form letter by letter, slowly building up a sentence (with a whooshing sound) while people in the audience wonder how they ended up here when they used to have such great hopes for their lives.

Just because these gimmicks are there, that doesn't mean you have to use them. Professional speakers don't. They know that the whizz-bang trickery is usually used to distract attention from the speaker and the fact that the slides themselves have nothing of value on them.

Keep things simple. The slides should be the focus, not the transitions between them.

That doesn't mean that you can't have movement on your slides if it's there for a purpose. For example, you can embed a video clip in a slide and play that. You can have an animated cartoon. You can include music if it's appropriate and there for a good reason. But don't do it just because you can.

Mistake 7: Including too much information on one slide

Visual aids should be big, bold and simple. They should make their point vividly and economically. They shouldn't be complicated or require a lot of thought to work out what they're saying.

Slides shouldn't really stand alone. The visual image works in partnership with your words to make the impact you want. Remember that your slides are not meant to be handouts. They're not meant to be printed off. So don't worry if they won't make sense to someone looking at them later who didn't come to the presentation.

Many slides end up with too much information on them, which makes them difficult to read and interpret. They also look incredibly boring. Why would anyone want to read them?

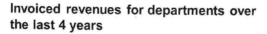

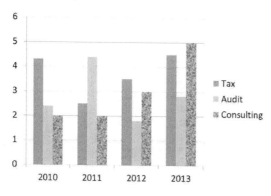

This sort of detailed information is best included, if at all, in supporting documentation such as a brief report which people can read later if they wish to.

As ever, it's best to work out exactly what point you want to make. For example, in the example above, do you just want to point out that Consulting has been steadily improving its performance and now brings in more money than any of the other departments? Once you've decided what you need to say, strip out anything which doesn't need to be there. It will only confuse people.

Mistake 8: Poor composition

It may have come as a surprise to you to find that your job involves speaking. It will come as even more of a surprise to find that you also need to be a graphic designer.

Well, that may be a bit of an exaggeration. But you do need to think about the design of your slides, how the various elements fit together and support each other, how you draw the viewer's eye to the most important aspects of the slide.

This could be one reason why a lot of business presenters just don't bother. They just use bullet points and avoid the issue altogether.

I'm not a graphic designer either, I must admit. All I want to offer you are some simple guidelines.

The most important one, and I know I've already mentioned this, is for you to be clear about what you want your slide to do. It should have one purpose, one message, and everything on it should support that message.

So you don't want so much on it that the audience are distracted, trying to figure out what to look at first or where their attention should be focused.

Think about the balance between picture and text. Their relative size and position should complement each other. If one is much bigger than the other it may dominate more than you want it to.

In this example, the text dominates and the image is too small, losing its impact.

Instead of having text separate from an image, try filling the slide with the image and then putting the text inside the image. This can be much more powerful and attractive. The only drawback might be that you may struggle to find a suitable colour for the text which makes it stand out against the picture. In that case, as in this example, you would have to put the text in a text box and shade in the background so it stands out.

Keeping Your Customers Happy

If you have a picture of a person on the slide as well as text, it will look better if you can arrange to have the person looking towards the text. This will draw people's eyes to the text as viewers naturally tend to follow the eye line of anyone they see in a picture.

Mistake 9: Not thinking enough about fonts

I readily accept that there are very few areas of your life where "Not thinking enough about fonts" will be a serious issue but this happens to be one of them.

I know I said not to show too many slides with words on, but some slides will probably have some words on so you do need to think about fonts. It matters.

Simply – don't use too many, make sure they're legible, make sure they give the impression you want.

Using lots of different fonts will look messy and confusing. Stick to one or two.

Serif fonts	Sans Serif fonts
Times New Roman	Arial
Georgia	Calibri
Book Antiqua	Century Gothic
Old English Text	Tahoma

As you can see from this example, some fonts are just easier to read than others. As a general rule, sans serif fonts are easier to read when written large than serif fonts. Serif fonts are ones like Times New Roman or Georgia, which have tails, feet or flicks. Sans serif fonts are simpler – like Arial, Calibri or Tahoma.

These are all easily available, which is why I mention them. People who design slides for a living probably avoid these and look for less popular alternatives but you probably have better things to do with your time than search around for obscure fonts, so stick to the usual ones. Just don't mix them all up and make sure, whatever you use, the size is big enough for people to read them from a distance.

One you probably want to avoid is Comic Sans.

Is this the right font to use for a serious message?

Of course, it depends on the impression you want to make. People who use Comic Sans tend to want to come over as informal, friendly, a little wacky or humorous (the clue's in the name).

That may be OK in some situations but, if you're in a business setting or speaking about a serious topic, it's probably not appropriate. It comes across like someone wearing a novelty tie with a business suit. It tries to say, "Hey look, I've got a sense of humour. I don't take myself too seriously." But actually it's just wrong.

Make sure people can read any words very easily, from all corners of the room you'll be speaking in.

This seems so obvious, but I've seen lots of presenters use slides which were impossible to read from more than a few feet away. The result was that people switched off completely and the presenter lost all credibility. After all, if you don't even make sure people can read the slides you're using, that doesn't suggest you've put a lot of thought into your presentation, does it?

This means that you need to see what your slides look like when run through a projector. Don't rely on just looking at them on your computer screen. If the presenters I mentioned above had taken the trouble to do this, they would have seen immediately that their slides were useless.

If possible, try out your slides in the actual room you'll be using, even if you just get there early and run through them before the presentation. I've found that slides which looked fine on my computer changed completely when run through a projector (compatibility problems, as the IT people always say). In some cases, the font sizes changed and I had to go back into the file and retype the text before I went on.

Mistake 10: Poor colour combinations

I can't show actual colour combinations here (I'm thinking of you - this book would cost you a lot more if it had colour pictures in) but be careful.

Generally, with text, use dark colours on a light background rather than light colours on a dark background. It's easier to read and easier on the eye.

> ## Light colours on a dark background

> ## Dark colours on a light background

If you're using a flipchart or whiteboard, avoid very light colours which won't show up well, such as pink, yellow or light blue. If I buy packs of flipchart pens in assorted colours,

I usually have to throw away at least 3 of them because they're no use. I don't know why the manufacturers keep making them.

Be careful with red and green, which can cause problems for some people with colour blindness. Don't use too many colours or combinations. Keep things simple.

Think about any associations people might make with colours – another problem with red and green. Red tends to signify danger or STOP, where green tends to suggest GO or something positive.

When you look at your visual aid, does the colour make one item stand out from the others? If so, was that your intention? If you don't want to draw attention to that item, change the colour.

What I said about checking fonts is also true of colours, by the way. Don't assume that what you see on your computer screen will be what you see when it's thrown up onto a screen. I've had colours change completely when I've connected my laptop or memory stick to a projector and had to go back and change them all manually while people were coming into the room for the talk. This is why you always need to turn up early before you speak. You'll be nervous enough without having to handle that sort of problem at the last minute.

Mistake 11: Using clichés

Where you have PowerPoint, you have ClipArt. It's so easy to insert pictures or photographs from the ClipArt collection that you might wonder why you would ever need to look elsewhere.

Well, because you want to be original and you don't want to use tired old pictures which everyone has seen before, that's why.

Your pictures should have an impact and that means you need to avoid images which other people have used and also avoid clichés.

By this I mean avoid the most obvious images. Probably the first image you think of will be a cliché (no offence, it's just that you're likely to think of the most obvious things first).

How To Succeed At Networking

Avoid using the picture everyone else would use, it looks as if you haven't put much thought into it. Try something a bit different, maybe something which puts a different slant on the topic.

Use original photos, cartoons, drawings, graphs, charts. There are lots of websites which provide images such as www.istockphoto.com or www.shutterstock.com You'll have to pay for the pictures but at least they're less likely to be ones which people have seen before.

If you go to one of these sites, you can type in a search term and see dozens, sometimes hundreds, of professionally produced photographs or illustrations. Sometimes just browsing through these can give you great ideas for images which you can use as metaphors or ways in which you could explain or structure your material that you hadn't thought of before. It's a good way to stimulate your creativity.

The other reason to use these sources is that their images usually come with rights to use them in a range of situations. You may not be aware, but you're not really supposed to use ClipArt images for commercial purposes. You're also not supposed to just download pictures from the internet unless they come with a specific licence allowing you to use them.

Just because images are in the public domain, e.g. someone's uploaded a video to YouTube, that doesn't mean you can use them. I've seen many presenters use clips from TV programmes or commercial films which they've downloaded from YouTube which I'm sure would infringe copyright law.

Mistake 12: Leaving the slide up when you're not talking about it

Remember that I said you shouldn't hide behind the visual aids. You should have people's attention focused on you when you don't have a visual to show them. Then, when you do have one, you direct their attention to it. Then, when you've finished with it, you take it away and draw their attention back to yourself.

Don't leave a slide up behind you when you've moved on to another point. It's just confusing and distracting for the audience and it looks as if you either haven't noticed or you just can't be bothered to keep up with your own talk.

If you're using a flipchart and you've prepared sheets to use, leave a blank sheet between them so you can turn over once you've talked about an image and just have the blank behind you.

If you're using PowerPoint, you can insert blank slides (i.e. just black or white) or just press the B key on your computer to black out the screen. Then press the B key again to reverse it or press the key (or click the remote) to move forward to your next slide. Alternatively, you can press W and get a white screen.

Chapter Six

How To Really Engage Your Audience

The success of any presentation or speech will depend on how much you really engage your audience.

Too many presentations consist of someone standing at the front speaking but making no real connection with the people they're speaking to. As far as the audience is concerned, it's just something that's going on in front of them, not something that involves them. So they can switch off, think about something else, start checking their text messages, it doesn't seem to matter.

But then there are some speakers who seem to be able to hold an audience's attention from start to finish. People are gripped, listening to every word, completely engaged and focused.

What makes the difference? That's what I'm about to reveal.

Say something worth listening to

A great deal of your success will depend, of course, on how you deliver your presentation and I'll say more about that shortly.

But what you actually say is also vital. And this goes right back to the beginning.

Remember, at the start of the book, I went through a 10 step plan for preparing a presentation? And that started with being clear about who you were speaking to and why? I said that, until you knew that, you couldn't start to prepare. You couldn't choose the right content without answering those questions – who and why?

If you've gone through that process, you should have chosen content which is relevant, interesting, pitched at the right level and of some benefit to the people you're speaking to.

That will get you a long way in terms of holding your audience's attention, even if your delivery isn't brilliant.

On the other hand, if your content is of no interest to people because it's irrelevant, too complex, too basic, too theoretical or because it's really all about what you want to tell them rather than what they need to know, then you're going to struggle.

Look and sound confident and competent

When you first step up to speak, the audience will be wondering if you're any good.

That may be blunt but it's true. They're hoping you're going to be good, after all they don't want to waste their time, but they're not sure (unless they've heard you before).

They want some reassurance, right at the start, that you know what you're doing. So your first impression needs to be a good one. Then you need to follow it up.

You can look confident by establishing eye contact, smiling and looking in control, especially at the start. This is not the time to be searching around for your notes or working out how to plug in the projector.

This is why it's important to be certain about what you're going to say at the very beginning. You need to make an impact, not be thinking of the right words or looking hesitant. I mentioned earlier some ways to open your talk, e.g. with a challenging statement, a quotation, a question.

Be aware that people may see you before you start speaking and will already have formed some judgement about you before you even open your mouth. If you're at the front as people come in, don't sit there looking terrified and only remembering to smile when you've stood up – it's too late. Look around the room confidently, not at anyone in particular, but not hiding your face. You'll look at ease and professional, however you happen to be feeling.

Similarly, if you're one of a panel of speakers, look as if you're listening to the people who are on before you. Don't switch off or sit there making notes or thinking about your own speech.

Dress in something which makes you feel comfortable but is at least as smart as your audience (so probably not shorts and flip-flops). Think about the impression you want to make.

When you stand up to speak, stand up straight with your feet comfortably apart and, initially, with your hands by your sides. If you're a man don't put your hands in your pockets. It looks too casual.

You'll soon move your hands naturally to gesture. If you must hold something, e.g. notes, still use one hand to gesture. Don't try to keep your hands still or you'll look unnatural.

Avoid fiddling with something in your hands while you speak. If you find yourself holding a pen, for instance, calmly put it down while you're speaking.

For your opening remarks, I suggest you stand still, making eye contact with people as you start to speak.

You can move around as you speak, so long as you move with purpose and don't just sway back and forth or pace up and down (this makes you look nervous) but, when you want to make an important point, stand still. It gives the point more impact and gravity.

Speak at a volume slightly higher than is necessary to reach the back row.

This will make sure everyone can hear and it will make you sound confident. It will cover any tremor in your voice and it will help to stop you saying things like " ...erm "

Use silence.

Pause to allow points to go home and to add emphasis. Seconds will seem like hours when you're up there, but it won't feel like that to your audience. You can easily stop talking for 5 seconds as a short pause.

Speak to people as if you're having a conversation

When you're having a conversation with someone, they don't usually tend to switch off and start doing something else, do they? If they do, you need to find some other topics of conversation.

A great presentation is a cross between a performance and a conversation. The more people you're speaking to and the larger the room, the more it becomes a performance because you can't just talk naturally to dozens (or hundreds) of people. Your voice, gestures and movements have to be bigger.

But the point of the performance is to give the *impression* of being a conversation.

By that I mean that every member of the audience needs to feel that you're speaking to him or her. They want to feel that you're talking *to* them, not talking *at* them. That's how they feel engaged.

Try to give the impression you're speaking to an individual – use normal expressions and sentences.

Use contractions, such as "I'll" and "we'll" if you want to sound less formal.

Break some of the rules of written grammar, such as ending sentences with prepositions or starting them with "and" or "but" (as I have in writing this book).

Use the active form rather than the passive. For example, say,

"We expect to make a profit of £3 million next year "

rather than,

"A profit of £3 million is expected for next year."

This is why writing the speech out in full first is not a good idea – you'll automatically use formal words and sentences which sound strange when spoken.

Face your audience and keep eye contact.

Not looking at the audience is the biggest mistake you can make. It's like giving them permission to switch off. And some people may slip out of the room if you don't keep an eye on them.

Also, eye contact will give you valuable feedback about how interested people are and whether they're following what you're saying. If they're reading newspapers or their eyes are closed, that's not a good sign.

Just keeping eye contact for a second with everyone will have a huge impact. Avoid staring at your own visual aids and, if you use notes, only glance at them.

With a small audience, keep looking around as you speak so that you engage everyone's attention. With a very large audience, you can look at a section and most people in that group will think you're looking at them. But don't just stare into space or look out over people's heads.

If it helps, look for someone friendly and attentive in the audience and glance at them from time to time to reassure yourself. But don't keep staring at them or they'll feel uncomfortable.

How long should you keep eye contact with someone? Up to 2 seconds is probably fine, 3 – 6 seconds and they'll think you *really* like them, more than that and they'll call the police.

Build rapport with your audience

Get the audience on your side from the start by building rapport with them.

What do I mean by rapport?

I mean:

- they like you

- they feel that you're concerned about them

- they feel that you understand them

- they feel that you have some empathy with them

- they feel that you're really trying to deliver something of benefit

If people feel you're trying and you're sincere, they'll put up with some things being less than perfect, they'll give you a chance.

How do you develop this rapport?

Be friendly and make eye contact with people from the start. Smile at them and talk to them as they come in if you can. Don't stand at the front arranging your notes or fiddling with the laptop, ignoring the audience.

Show that you understand their concerns and their needs by setting out exactly how the talk will help them.

Make them feel special.

Avoid giving people the feeling that this is the tenth time you've given this talk, even if it is. People don't want to see you going through the motions, looking tired or bored with your own presentation, or giving them some generic information which isn't geared towards their own situations.

Show that you have something in common with them. People tend to like people who are like them. You can do this by sharing some experiences you've had which are similar to theirs, especially challenges.

Don't make things up, be authentic, but find areas in common if they exist.

Don't take yourself too seriously. Tell some stories about things that have happened to you which show that you can laugh at yourself (so long as they're relevant).

Don't go too far, you don't want to make yourself look like an idiot! But a few references to times when you made a bit of a mess of things can help to make you look more human and show that you don't think you're perfect.

Appeal to different types of people

You need to understand that people have different ways of seeing the world, they have different needs and they react differently to ideas and suggestions.

There isn't room here to go into all the possible variations. People's reactions to anything you say will be determined by their beliefs and values which, in turn, can be affected by their family background, their education, their cultural environment, their experiences, their past relationships and a host of other factors.

You can't be expected to know how everyone in your audience may differ from the person sitting next to them. Just be aware that these differences exist, which means that not everyone will respond in the same way you would to anything you say or do.

If you want to get this fixed in your mind, just think PANTS.

That stands for **P**eople **A**re **N**ot **T**he **S**ame.

Here are just a couple of very broad examples.

I would suggest many people can be divided into Pain-killers or Pleasure-seekers.

Pain-killers are people who are motivated mainly by the need to avoid pain. They like to stay as they are, they don't like the thought of change or of having to handle anything new. They have a definite comfort zone and they feel anxious if they're forced out of it.

They tend to take action only if there is a prospect of feeling pain if they don't. In other words, if it will be more painful to stay as they are than to change. So, if you're suggesting some new process or way of doing things (e.g. introducing a new software system), these people will be reluctant and resistant. They won't respond to promises of how wonderful the world will be when these changes have come through.

You need to deal with their anxiety about the change, reassure them about how easy it will be to adapt to the new system and also suggest that things will get worse without this change and their lives will somehow become more difficult.

Pleasure-seekers, on the other hand, are always on the lookout for something new. They like change, they have a sense of adventure and will try anything if it promises to make their lives better. They're like the "early adopters" of new technology, the first ones to have the new phone or computer.

They can be driven by a vision of a future which is shiny and new. So, if you're introducing a new system to these people, focus on how it will make everything quicker and easier and make sure it seems "cutting edge" and ahead of the competition.

People also differ in terms of how much they need logic and reason to support an argument and how much they respond to emotion and feeling.

So, if you're trying to persuade people to do something, make sure you include a mixture of all these things. For people who respond to logic and reason, you'll need lots of detail and well-supported arguments to persuade them to make a decision or take an action.

Others go on what "feels right" to them. So you appeal to those people with more emotional arguments or perhaps appealing to their sense of what's right.

In the end, we all take decisions based on a mixture of reason and emotion, so try to cover both in some way in your presentation.

These are just a few examples of how people differ. My advice to you is, firstly, to find out as much as you can about the people you're speaking to (did I mention that?) and don't make assumptions about them. Then try to deliver your key messages in a variety of ways so that they will engage, and have an impact on, different types of people.

Tell stories

Stories are a great way to get your point across and to engage an audience.

Stories draw people in. We all love a good story. We spend most of our time telling each other stories, stories about what has happened to us during the day, what we've seen and done, what our friends and family have been up to. We read stories in the newspapers and watch stories on the television.

So, as a presenter, weaving your material around stories is a wonderful way of engaging your audience. People can follow a story, they can relate to the people in it and, crucially, they can remember it more easily than a series of facts and figures.

For the same reasons, using stories can also help you to remember your key themes and points and to simplify the structure of your talk. If you can build your message around a story, or a group of stories, then you'll find it has a natural flow and a sequence which you can easily follow.

Get people involved

One of the reasons why people switch off when they're listening to a presentation, and why speakers have to work so hard to keep their attention, is because there really isn't much for them to do. They just have to sit there and listen.

So one way to keep the audience engaged is by actually involving them, by making the presentation more interactive.

I say more about this in the chapter on how to help people understand and remember information because it's also very important in terms of helping people to learn. But here are just a few ways to get your audience involved and make it more of a dialogue than a monologue.

Ask for a simple show of hands in response to something you've said.

Ask the audience questions – simple but effective.

Ask people to talk to the person next to them or discuss a point in a small group, then ask for ideas or contributions.

Or ask them to discuss any questions they have about what you've said. Bear in mind that, if you've set them off in discussion, you may need something to make a noise in order to get their attention again e.g. a bell, whistle or duck call.

Ask people to give you examples to illustrate points you've made, drawn from personal experiences, e.g. "the worst...", "the best...".

Ask people to write something down individually if the group is too big. For example, "write down one thing you could do to put this idea into practice." This makes them think more about the material. Then ask for some ideas.

Hand out a quick quiz about some of the material you've covered. This could be pictograms or puzzles. Use this as a short break during the talk.

Give out cards and ask people to write down any questions that arise which you haven't answered. Have a short break, collect the cards in and pick out some of the most useful questions. Answer them in the next session.

Use some "tricks of the trade"

Really good speakers use a number of techniques to keep their presentations lively, interesting, vivid and engaging. Here are a few which you can use to have your audience hanging on your every word.

Use relevant quotations.

Quotations can be a great way to open a presentation with impact. You can use them to raise questions in people's minds, to challenge their thinking or to make them curious.

For example, if you were talking about teaching or training, you might open with the following statement:

"I never teach my pupils. I only attempt to provide the conditions in which they can learn." Albert Einstein

You could then build your talk around it, expanding on it or examining the arguments for and against it.

Avoid the most obvious people and the ones everyone has heard before. Or see if you can use a well – known quotation but in a different context to give it a new twist.

Use rhetorical questions, such as, "So what does that mean for people such as yourselves? How will your lives be changed if this proposal goes through?"

The power of these questions, if used well, is that people automatically think about the answer in their heads. Then they want to hear your answer, which you are, of course, about to deliver.

Use repetition of a particular phrase to build emphasis. "Is it right that we should have no say in this? Is it right that we should be expected to accept it with no consultation?" (Notice the use of rhetorical questions!)

Use the power of three. "This software has the power to change the way you work, change the way you communicate, change the way you do business."

Three times seems enough to build to a climax without overdoing it.

Bring in startling statistics, "Every 5 minutes, someone trips over a cat." (But don't make them up, like I just did)

How to use lecterns and microphones and still connect with the audience

Many presenters make some basic errors when faced with a lectern or when asked to use a microphone which can seriously affect their ability to connect with the audience. So here are a few tips

If you're faced with a lectern, don't feel obliged to use it.

Sometimes people just put them there because they think that's what speakers want. In some cases you'll have little choice because of the layout of the room but, if you can stand away from it and give your presentation just as easily, do so. You'll look more relaxed and will contrast well with any previous speakers who have stood behind it.

Having said that, some people do manage to use one without letting it interfere with the impact of their talk.

If you do use it, just be aware that you'll need to work extra hard to avoid looking like you're giving a lecture.

Look out over the top of the lectern at the audience and resist the temptation to look down at your notes constantly.

Don't cling to the sides of the lectern with white knuckles like a drowning man clutching onto driftwood.

If you're using a microphone, speak at the sort of volume you would use if you were talking to the people in the first few rows and everyone should be able to hear you without your being too loud.

And test any microphone first. Check how to switch it on and off and WHO will switch it on before you start.

A microphone on a stand, or a free – held one, will usually be switched on at the microphone itself.

A lapel microphone usually requires you to wear a pack clipped onto your person (e.g. on a belt) and it will need to be switched on at the pack rather than at the microphone.

If it's on a stand, make sure you know whether you have to speak directly into it and, if so, you will have to adapt your delivery to stop yourself looking away from it.

Given the choice, always go for a lapel microphone as this gives you much more freedom to walk around and speak naturally. Just pin it somewhere so it won't pick up rustling sounds when you move.

And please remember to turn it off when you stop speaking – you don't want everyone to hear you saying, "Thank goodness that's over. What a miserable audience."

Chapter Seven

How To Help People Understand And Remember

In the days when I was a Tax Consultant, I spent quite a few years delivering presentations to colleagues and clients. I travelled all round the UK and parts of Europe speaking about Tax.

You might think of Tax as a boring subject but I loved it. There were lots of interesting stories to tell about the schemes people had come up with and the weird things judges had said in determining Tax cases in the courts.

That's where I learned a lot about how to convert complicated legislation into content which was interesting, engaging, clear and easy to understand.

I worked with some very creative and imaginative people who came up with great ideas to make their content accessible and entertaining.

But I also saw a lot of presenters who never quite "got" the idea that they were supposed to make their material interesting and easy to follow. Either that, or they just had no idea how to do it. They were clearly experts but they often failed to get their own knowledge across to their audiences. They left people bored, baffled or both.

If you've ever sat through an excruciating PowerPoint-driven talk which lost your interest and confused you after the first 5 minutes, you'll know exactly what I mean.

Why do technical people struggle?

Some of the reasons why technical people or subject specialists often struggle are:

- they often have little, or no, knowledge of how to help people understand and remember information

- they're not skilled speakers – why should they be, that's not what they're good at

- they're often people who have learned their subjects quite easily and so don't always understand how other people can struggle to grasp the ideas

- for that reason, they don't know how to explain themselves in simple terms

- they tend to be a bit fanatical about their own subject areas and assume that other people will want, and need, to know everything about them so they overload their sessions with too much content

And it's not really their fault. Often, they receive little or no training in how to present information. They have to do their best while, at the same time, doing their other work.

So here are some key tips on how to help your audiences understand and remember the information you're giving them.

Give them a reason to pay attention

People are bombarded with information every hour of the day. Do you think they remember all they see and hear? Of course not.

How many people do you see in a day? How many cars? How many houses? How many do you notice and remember? Not many.

The brain filters out a lot of the "white noise" in the background, all the information it receives which it doesn't perceive to be important.

On the other hand, if you have a particular interest in something, guess what happens? You notice it, you pay attention to it, you remember anything associated with it.

For example, I'm really interested in football and find I can easily remember all sorts of trivia about football (results, scorers, goals) even without making the slightest effort.

If you decide to change your car, as I did recently, and you have a couple of models in mind, you'll start seeing those cars everywhere.

We all pick out and remember things we've tagged as being important us and we tend to blank out the rest. Think about what this means for your presentation. Is the information you're delivering part of the essential, "tagged as important" stuff for your audience or is part of the "white noise" which they feel they can safely ignore?

Make sure you tell them as soon as you can how important your topic is to them and how it's going to affect them so they see it as something worth paying attention to.

Don't have too much content

Yes, I know I've mentioned this before. I make no apologies for it.

I'll say it again - many presentations are ruined by being overloaded with content because the people who designed them weren't thorough enough in finding out about their audience and weren't ruthless enough in stripping out redundant content.

How much do people really need to know at this stage? What are the essential points they have to learn if the presentation is to be successful?

For example, people who work on the counter in banks serving the public need to know a lot about many of the products the banks sell so they can spot opportunities to offer them to customers.

But they don't necessarily have to know everything about them. They don't need to know every last detail.

Someone else, who specialises in those products, needs to know that, but the people on the counter probably need to know just enough to understand who the products are aimed at so they can pick out relevant people to mention the products to and to refer them to the experts when the situation arises.

If the person delivering a presentation to these people doesn't understand why they need it and what they're going to do with the information, they'll probably put in too much detail. They'll include material that maybe only the experts really need to know because they haven't thought through who the presentation is aimed at and what those people need.

Another question to ask yourself is, do people actually need to remember lots of information or do they just need to know it's there and where to find it when they need it?

As in the example of the bank staff, often the main thing is that people know enough to spot the situations where they have to take some action, then they need to know where the detailed information is, or who to refer to, if the situation arises.

Start from people's existing knowledge.

Start from what people already know and link new information to that.

One of the ways that the brain learns is by forming connections between new information and what it already knows. If you help people to make those connections, you'll be helping them to understand and to remember more successfully.

If you connect with something they already know, they'll also feel more confident that this isn't something entirely new to them. On a common sense level, you need to start from where people are and lead them to the level of knowledge that you want them to have. If you start two steps ahead of them, they'll never catch up.

That might sound obvious but it's not always done. It's tempting, when you're starting a presentation to just think, "Right, let's get on with it " and to dive straight into the new material without referring back to anything the audience have done before or setting out how what you're going to cover fits in with what they already know.

And sometimes we make assumptions about what people know without necessarily checking whether this is right. You need to know as much as you can about your audience before you begin preparing your content (a point I may have mentioned already once or twice).

Even if you're talking to people about an area you think is brand new to them, you can still find ways to connect it to things they have already come across.

When I trained people in the details of Inheritance Tax, for instance, I'd start by talking about situations they might have met or heard about, such as people being left something in a will or stories in the papers they might have seen. This brings the material to life and, as I've said, it helps them to feel relaxed and confident about it because they can relate it to something they already know about, it's not entirely foreign to them.

Use stories and real life examples as much as possible.

I've mentioned using stories as a way of engaging with your audience. They are also a great way of helping people to understand and remember information.

It's often hard to grasp very technical information because it can seem to be divorced from real life situations. It's just a lot of detail, jargon or figures. Do what you can to bring it to life and make it real by telling stories or describing real situations that are relevant to the material.

If you're dealing with Health and Safety legislation, for example, there must be plenty of horror stories you can tell about accidents that have happened to people that will illustrate why certain rules are necessary.

If you're talking to people about financial products, tell them what sort of people will use those products, describe clients you've worked with, situations where people have used the products and the difference they've made.

If you're training people to use a system or a process, tell them about things that have gone wrong in the past because people didn't know how to use the system properly.

This adds interest, it helps people to see the point of what you're talking about and it certainly helps people to remember. Stories are really powerful ways to fix something in the memory. Think about how you pass on news or information to your friends. You tell them stories about what you've been doing. We all like to hear stories and we recall them much more easily than isolated pieces of information.

Start from the general before you move to the specific.

I mentioned that people learn by making connections between new information and what they already know. One way you can make this easier for them is to give them the big picture, the context, before you go into any level of detail.

When there's a foreign news item on the television, the presenter might say, "And here's our correspondent in Kabul." If they think you might not be sure where that is, they might show a map of the general area first, zooming in on Afghanistan, then pinpointing Kabul so you get a sense of where they're taking you.

That's what you need to do for your audience. Don't plunge straight into detail, lead them into it gently.

This does several things. It reminds people of what they already know, which I mentioned earlier. It warms them up for the presentation in the same sort of way you would warm up before you take exercise, you wouldn't just go out and start running as fast as you can, you would warm up gently first, then increase your speed. Giving people the context also helps them to focus their attention, to get used to the fact that they're about to learn something and to see where the new material fits in. Give people several opportunities to hear and remember the key points.

You can't just tell people something once and expect them to remember it. They may not even hear it or understand it the first time around. You need to build in repetition to make sure information gets heard and remembered.

Right at the start of your presentation, give people an overview of what you're going to cover, tell them the key things they'll learn. This isn't quite the same as giving them the big picture which I've just mentioned. That's more a way of setting the context for them. What I mean here is a bit like the Contents page of a book. You're going through what they're going to learn.

In the same way as, when you read the Contents page of a book, it's preparing you for what's coming, you're doing the same thing here. You're preparing people, you're signposting the main points that are coming so that, first of all, they'll find it easier to follow you, but also they'll spot the key points more easily when they arise and they'll remember them more effectively.

You might even get people to think of some questions they might have about the material and to write these down, then point out when you get to the parts where you answer these questions. Again, you're preparing people.

Going back to the example of reading a book, if you open a book looking for the answer to a question, you tend to notice and pick out the sections that answer your question. You had a purpose when you opened the book, you didn't just start reading, hoping something useful might come up.

Another way of doing this is to have "fill in the gaps" workbooks that people follow as you go along, with spaces in for them to write down points as you get to them. This helps them to focus and remember.

Then you need to build in repetition and recaps as you go along. Present information in different ways so that you repeat points without just saying them over and over again, for example using visual aids, quizzes, case studies, questions, whatever ways you can find to repeat your points so that people have several chances to understand them.

And, at the end, go over what you've covered and have a final recap before you finish.

It's like the old saying, tell them what you're going to tell them, tell them, then tell them what you've told them. It does actually make sense, it's a great way to help people understand and remember.

Be positive and enthusiastic about your subject

Take steps to get your audience in a positive frame of mind about the material you're presenting before you start.

If you're talking about some technical information or something new to the audience, they may well have negative expectations, thinking it's going to be difficult or boring. They might feel that they're going to struggle with it, or that they'll be confused. You need to change that by being very positive about it yourself.

Avoid negative language, such as, "This is quite a tricky area" or, "You might find this difficult." And certainly don't say, "I know this isn't very interesting."

You may think it's helpful to warn people, but you're setting up negative expectations about the subject. If you tell people something is going to be difficult, they'll feel less confident about approaching the material and they will expect to struggle (and they probably will).

Also, make sure you're not feeling negative about it yourself. If you think it's boring or difficult, that's bound to come across to your audience, they'll pick it up from you. And, after all, it's your job to make the material interesting and accessible. Don't blame the material for being difficult or dull. There is no dull material, just dull presenters.

If you can, send out material before the presentation. Stress the benefits of the talk, tell people what they'll be able to do after it, present it as an opportunity that they shouldn't miss, not a chore that they have to go through.

People who are anxious, worried or reluctant aren't in the right frame of mind to take in information. If you think people might be reluctant to be there, or anxious about what they're going to hear, you need to work twice as hard to reassure them and to make them feel positive and optimistic about it.

Use a variety of methods to deliver your material

People don't all take in information or learn in the same way. We all tend to develop certain preferences for the way we do these things. There are lots of models and theories about this area but the general point is that people are different. (Remember I mentioned PANTS in the chapter on how to engage with your audience?)

Remember that your training needs to appeal to people with different preferences. Don't use just one approach to present your material.

Also, we all take in information better if it is presented in a variety of ways and engages more of our senses.

You can use visual aids to present information in the form of pictures, diagrams, charts, graphs, video clips or other images (see the chapter on using visual aids for more detail).

Obviously, you will be speaking (unless you try to deliver your presentation through the medium of mime) so you will be engaging people's sense of hearing as well. Help them follow your verbal explanations by explaining your points clearly using some of the techniques set out in this chapter and elsewhere in this book.

Ideally, give people an opportunity to be physically active, to move around or to get hold of things and use them in order to learn. This engages other senses and also gets your audience much more involved in the process.

Some people need time for individual reflection to take things in and work them out, others need group discussion, a chance to interact with their colleagues. Find ways to build time into your presentation for these activities – the chapter on engaging with your audience will give you some tips on how to make your talks more interactive.

Use group work and pair work to let people discuss what they've heard. Get people moving around so they're not just sitting in the same place all the time listening to you. As well as making sure your presentation more appealing, it's actually easier for you than having to stand at the front talking all the time. It gives you a bit of a break.

(If you're involved in training and you want to learn how to deliver interactive workshops rather than just presenting information, you should have a look at my other book, "How To Design And Deliver Great Training", available from Amazon.)

Avoid jargon

I remember one day, when I was a Tax consultant, standing in the office when one of the Partners came out. He called over to a young man who had recently joined the department. He said, "David, come into my office and bring your Bible with you. I want to have a chat about CFCs."

The young man looked around in confusion. The only CFCs he knew about were those things in aerosols which are bad for the environment. And why would he need a Bible to talk about them?

In fact, CFCs in this case meant Controlled Foreign Companies (an important issue in international Tax planning in those days) and "the Bible" was the way people in the department referred to the huge volume of Tax legislation which we all carried around with us back then. This was a great example of jargon at work.

All professions have jargon, whether it's doctors and politicians or teachers and accountants.

Jargon is like a private language. It's a language we all speak and yet don't understand. What I mean is, we all speak our own jargon but we don't understand other people's.

And that's the point. Jargon is only "jargon" to an outsider. To insiders it's a form of shorthand. It depends on their shared knowledge and understanding. Within their own group it's not a problem, but when they have to communicate with other people it causes difficulty.

If you're giving a presentation to people who aren't specialists in your field, you need to make a real effort to avoid jargon.

Part of the problem is we are so used to using these terms to the people we work with that we often don't even realise we're doing it when we speak or write to someone else.

The main way to avoid it is to keep in mind who you're speaking to. Try to put yourself in the place of someone who is a complete outsider to your world.

If possible, get someone who isn't a specialist to look at your notes or listen to you go through the presentation. Sometimes a secretary or PA can do this for you. Often they will recognise terms they have to type regularly but they don't actually know what they mean. Ask them to read or listen to something and pick out any words they don't understand. Or use someone in a different department to your own.

Bring statistics to life

If you're giving people statistics or other technical information, think about how to turn this into something which is easily understood. One way is to use visual aids, as I've mentioned elsewhere.

Present statistics in visual form using simple bar charts or visual comparisons.

For example, if you're comparing alcohol consumption in different countries (I don't know why I thought of that one) you could represent each country with a bottle and have different sized bottles to show the differences in the figures.

Make sure you keep such visuals simple and clear and don't put too much information into them.

Another way to help people understand figures or statistics is to use familiar references and comparisons. For example:

"That's about the size of 3 tennis courts."

"That's the equivalent of a human being jumping over a skyscraper."

"This tiny memory stick can hold as many books as your local library."

If you do this, make sure you use references which people will actually be familiar with and which will make sense to them.

News reports in the UK often seem to use the size of Wales as a guide when reporting on events in other parts of the world. Reporters will say, "An area the size of Wales was devastated..." or, "Each year, an area of rainforest the size of Wales is cut down..." I don't know why they think everyone in the UK has a clear idea of the size of Wales. And I'm not sure how the people of Wales feel about being used as a comparison whenever something bad happens.

Chapter

Eight

How To Handle Questions

When do you want people to ask questions?

Tell the audience whether you want questions during the talk or at the end.

If you're running a very informal, participative session then you should expect, and welcome, questions at any time.

However if, say, you're explaining some very technical area or you're not feeling too confident and you think questions might throw you, you may want to leave questions until the end. You might also be concerned that taking questions will disrupt your timing (which it will, unless you're very flexible).

The danger with leaving questions until the end is that people tend to want to ask questions when they first think of them. If they think of a question, it's a sign that there's something they need to know. If they don't have a chance to ask their question, it may just distract them or prevent them from following the rest of the presentation.

Whichever approach you choose, here are some tips for handling questions.

How to ask for questions

Some people have perfected a technique of asking for questions in a way which is almost guaranteed to make sure that no-one asks one.

You've probably seen them, if you haven't used them yourself.

For example:

"Well, that's about it. That's the end of the talk but, before we all go, does anyone have a question?"

(In other words, "Does anyone want to annoy the rest of the group by holding them up?")

"So there you are. I think that's all pretty straightforward, but does anyone have a question?"

(In other words, "Is anyone so stupid that they didn't understand what I just said?")

If you really want people to ask questions, you need to look as if you mean it when you ask for them.

People need time to frame their questions. They need to decide whether they do have a question and then whether they want to ask it.

This can take several seconds, during which you should just stop talking and look around the group, showing that you're prepared to wait. Don't look as if you're in a hurry to get on, look as if you're really keen to get a question from someone.

The words you use when you ask for questions can also make a difference.

The classic, "So...any questions?" is not usually very productive.

You can make your appeal more inviting by saying something like, "Who has a question?" or, "What questions do you have?"

Both these approaches imply that there must be some questions and you want to find out what they are.

You could take it even further and say, "We've covered a lot of material here. I'm sure you must have some questions about some of the areas we've discussed. This is your chance to ask them. Who would like to start?"

Handling the questions you get

When you do get a question, follow these simple rules:

- Repeat any question you're asked to make sure everyone hears it.

  It's really irritating for a group to be listening to your answer to a question they never heard.

  Repeating the question also allows you to check that you've heard it correctly and may give you a chance to slightly rephrase it if you're not sure about it.

- When you answer a question, talk to the whole audience, not just the person who asked it, or others may switch off. Once a question is asked, it becomes the property of the whole room.

  Avoid getting drawn into a discussion with one person. If they want to keep following up their question, ask them to talk to you later.

- If you don't know the answer to a question, say something like, "That's an interesting question, I haven't come across that situation" rather than just, "I've no idea". If you can't think of an answer yourself, refer it to the rest of the audience to see if anyone else knows.

Don't always feel obliged to tell someone you'll look up the answer and get back to them.

This can cause you hours of work later. Try saying, "That's a good point to raise. If you find the answer, I'd be very interested to hear it."

- If you're asked a question which is off the topic, don't get drawn in.

Say something like, "That's a good question, but I didn't really want to go into that area in this talk. I'd be happy to discuss it with you later."

If you set out clearly the scope of your talk at the start, it makes this approach easier.

- Stay in control of the question period.

Keep the time limited and restrict the number of questions. Many talks fade away at this point as people get restless and start looking at their watches. Then the only thing they remember is how long the question session went on.

If the question session has gone on for some time, you may want to repeat your summary very briefly so people are reminded of your own key points.

Chapter Nine

The End Is Nigh

In fact, here it is.

What you've just read (I hope you did read it, you didn't just skip to the back to see how it ended, did you?) is a collection of just about every useful point I can think of from many years of public speaking and running courses on Presentation Skills.

I guarantee, if you can put these into practice you'll be an outstanding speaker—the sort that people will make a point of going to listen to.

But *practice* is the word. There are no more secrets. You can buy all the books in the world—in the end, it's down to you. Go out there and speak to people, try out some of these ideas and perfect your technique.

Take every opportunity to speak and to watch and listen to other speakers. Keep an eye out for what works and what doesn't. Shamelessly steal good ideas (everyone does it) and learn from bad experiences.

I wish you the best of luck!

And remember, if you would like to arrange a course on Presentation Skills for your organisation, or have individual coaching, please give me a call.

How I Can Help You And Your Organisation

Whether you:

- deliver business or academic presentations

- address meetings

- speak to conferences

- talk to clients

- deliver sales pitches or tenders

- lead seminars or training events

here's what I'll do for you.

I'll help you craft a clear and compelling message and deliver it with impact.

I'll give you proven tips and techniques based on 40 years of public speaking, using "insider" knowledge to help you speak like a professional.

Training

- In-house training for businesses or organisations

- Specifically designed to suit your needs, your business, your people

- Covering all aspects from initial preparation to design to delivery

- Lively, engaging, interactive, fun – but always practical

Coaching

- Working with individuals to develop skills or to prepare a specific presentation

- Reviewing slides, structure, materials, etc. to craft a powerful presentation

- Helping to build confidence and presence

- Watching presentations and giving detailed feedback

- Face to face or with phone or Skype support

Visit the website at:

http://www.TransformYourPresentations.com

for more information

Also by

Alan Matthews

How To Design And Deliver Great Training

"This book is excellent. I wish it had been around years ago when I first took training sessions." Sue Pullen

Do you deliver training in technical or academic subjects?

You may be a great presenter, but when you're trying to help people learn and remember information, that's not enough. You need to know the different ways people learn. You need to know how the brain works. You need to know how to support learners by providing engaging activities and a stimulating environment.

"I absolutely adore your book. I have been training now for 12 years and this is the most readable book I've come across." Tammy Harper

How do you turn dry or complex material into exciting, interactive and effective training?

How do you turn reluctant participants into willing, enthusiastic learners?

How do you use questions, activities and creative visual aids to engage your learners and help them remember your key points?

This practical, easy-to-read book will reveal all.

"Alan has come up with a must-have book for all trainers, both new and experienced." Alison Reeves

Whether you are a part-time trainer, a subject specialist who has to combine training with your "proper job" or an experienced trainer, you will find this book invaluable.

Available on Amazon – read the 5 star reviews and order your copy!

About
The
Author

I'm a trainer, coach and speaker based in Solihull in the UK.

I've been a public speaker for over 40 years (I started young). I've spoken to conferences, business seminars, public meetings and, if no—one else is around, I often talk to myself.

I'm one of those strange people who loves speaking in public. I've even won competitions in public speaking (although, let's face it, who in their right mind would even *enter* a competition in public speaking?)

I've been involved in learning and development for over 20 years, specialising in helping people to develop excellent communication skills and to increase the impact they have on others.

In this time, I've helped hundreds of people to improve their presentation skills through workshops and individual coaching.

I'm available to run in-house training courses, to work one to one with individuals or to speak to meetings or conferences about communication, personal impact or training and development. Visit the website at

www.TransformYourPresentations.com

for more details of how I can help you or your organisation.

You can also download free articles and reports from the website and join my mailing list to receive regular newsletters to help you to deliver outstanding presentations.

Contact Details: Alan Matthews

Phone: 01564 770436

Website: www.transformyourpresentations.com

Email: alan@transformyourpresentations.com

Made in the USA
Charleston, SC
08 March 2016